Digital Art for Teenagers
Introductory Techniques

Table of Contents

Chapter 1. Introduction

Immerse yourself in the vibrant and thrilling world of Digital Art for Teenagers: Introductory Techniques! This Special Report is your golden ticket into the world of digital creativity! Whether you are just starting out or looking to sharpen your skills, our comprehensive guide is tailored to help young artists navigate this dazzling universe. Brighten up your world with our stepping-stones to digital masterpieces, be it bold manga characters, mesmerizing landscapes, captivating animations, or more! Smile and unlock your artistic potentials hidden in those fingertips. Order this Special Report, and let's embark on this inspiring painting journey together. Start nurturing that spark of creativity today because Picasso once said, "art washes away from the soul the dust of everyday life". Get ready to scrub up your soul with a swirl of our digital paint! Let's ignite the spark for art!

Chapter 2. Understanding Digital Art: Fundamentals and Scope

The world of digital art opens up a galaxy of fun and creativity. You may think of it as drawing on a computer, but it's so much more than that. It's about bringing your imagination to life with the aid of today's technological tools.

2.1. Understanding Digital Art

Digital art is a general term for a range of artistic works and practices that use digital technology as an essential part of the creative or presentation process. Since the 1960s, various names have been used to describe this phenomenon, such as computer art and multimedia art, with digital art itself being placed under the larger umbrella term of new media art.

Depending on the artist's intention, the output of digital art can be presented on many platforms, ranging from digital screens to projections on buildings or the creation of physical objects through 3D printing. It also integrates various digital elements from other sources like photo manipulations, graphic design elements, or even sound design.

Some people may argue that digital art is not real art because it's done on a computer. But any tool used to create art requires skill. The computer is just another medium, like a canvas, clay, or watercolors. What truly matters is the idea, the emotion, and the piece's ability to communicate the artist's message to the viewer.

2.2. The Fundamentals of Digital Art

Before embarking on your journey in the digital art universe, there are some basic elements and principles you need to understand.

2.2.1. Elements of Digital Art

Elements of art are the building blocks of creating a visual piece. They are what you use to create your artistic piece on your digital platform. These include:

- Line: The first and most basic element of art. It can be thick, thin, wavy, straight, or of various colors. It is used to create shapes, contours, and outlines.

- Shape: This refers to the closed lines that are 2-dimensional (length and height). These shapes can be geometric, like circles and squares, or organic, which are typically irregular or uneven.

- Color: Digital art gives you an unlimited palette! Understanding color theories, such as warm versus cool colors or complementary colors, can strengthen your artwork.

- Texture: This is the surface quality that can be seen or felt. With digital art, you can create perceived texture that viewers instinctively 'feel' with their eyes.

- Space: This refers to the area in which art is organized. It may have two dimensions (length and width) or three dimensions (length, width, and height).

- Form: Any three-dimensional object that can be measured by length, width, and depth.

- Value: The lightness or darkness of a color.

2.2.2. Principles of Digital Art

The principles of art help you arrange the elements in a way that guides the viewer's eye around the whole piece. These principles are:

- Balance: The distribution of visual weight in a piece. It can be symmetrical, asymmetrical, or radial.

- Contrast: Deals with the difference in elements. It could be dark versus light, or the juxtaposition of textures.

- Emphasis: This is what catches the viewer's eye. It's what the artist uses to create interest or convey the most important part of the artwork.

- Movement: How the viewer's eye travels through the piece, guided by lines, shapes, and colors.

- Rhythm: The visual beat, achieved by repeating certain elements to create a sense of unity and balance.

- Unity: Occurs when all parts of the artwork combine to create a balanced, harmonious complete piece.

- Proportion: The relative size of elements within the artwork.

Understanding these foundational theories will help you harness the power of your digital tools more effectively.

2.3. Scope of Digital Art

With the rapid technological advancements, digital art has found its applications in numerous fields. It's not just limited to creating art for art's sake but is also heavily implemented in many industries.

One major field is the entertainment industry, where digital art is used in film, television, video games and even theatre productions. Whether it's creating fantastic creatures, lush environments, or designing the graphic interface for a video game, digital art is crucial.

Another key field is advertising and marketing. Digital artists can create everything from captivating banners and posters to comprehensive brand identity packages.

In the field of fashion, digital art is used in designing patterns, creating virtual fashion shows, and even in the designing of clothes through digital techniques.

Moreover, architecture and interior design leverage digital art through CGI and 3D rendering to create realistic design plans and virtual tours.

The world of digital art is broad and limitless. Understanding these fundamentals and scope will provide a greater foundation from where you can explore, improve, and eventually excel. The most important thing to remember is have fun as that is the true essence of any art form.

Chapter 3. Decoding Art Software: A Guide to The Most Popular Tools

Digital art has transformed the way we create, allowing endless possibilities for artists to express their creativity. One of the key components of digital art is the software used to create it. There are a wide variety of art softwares available today, each with its distinct features and tools. This section will break down some of the most popular art software in the market to help you decide which one might be the most suitable for your artistic endeavors.

3.1. Understanding the Basics

Before deep-diving into the specifics of each software, it's crucial to understand the ABCs of digital art software. Essentially, these applications serve as your digital canvas and toolset, allowing you to produce art pieces on an electronic platform. Typically, you would draw with a stylus on a graphics tablet, which translates your strokes into digital form. Some software also comes with tools for 3D modeling and animation.

3.2. Adobe Photoshop

Perhaps the most commonly known digital art software is Adobe Photoshop. Photoshop is not just for photo editing; it's also a versatile tool for creating digital art. With a myriad of brushes, textures, and effects, Photoshop offers a high level of customization. It supports layers and has adjustment options for luminosity, color balance, and experiment with blend modes. You can add depth and detail to your art with its powerful filters and transformation tools. Photoshop is preferred by seasoned artists for its advanced features and granular control. However, it might not be very beginner-friendly due to its somewhat complex interface.

3.3. Procreate

Exclusively for iPad users, Procreate is a digital painting app that many professional artists swear by. It offers an intuitive interface, and you can use Apple Pencil for finer control. Procreate offers over 130 brushes, a layer system, an extensive color palette, and various effects. Its ability to replicate the feel of traditional media like pencils, inks, charcoal, and more is highly acclaimed. Moreover, its 'Streamline' feature guarantees smoother strokes, making it perfect for practicing calligraphy.

3.4. Krita

Krita is a free software that matches premium software in terms of capabilities. Highly recommended for comic and manga artists, Krita offers customizable templates for typical comic formats. It also comes loaded with a wide array of brushes and supports creating custom ones. It has an excellent layer management system along with a multibrush tool for creating more complex 3D artwork. The only downside is that it has a high learning curve for beginners.

3.5. Autodesk SketchBook

Another fantastic tool for beginners is Autodesk SketchBook. With its intuitive interface and a focus on drawing and concept sketching, it's a great software to master the basics. It offers a distraction-free drawing environment with tools for creating simple sketches to detailed works of art. SketchBook also has a unique feature called the "Copic Color Library", beloved by artists for its vibrance and accuracy.

3.6. Clip Studio Paint

Clip Studio Paint, earlier known as Manga Studio, is a software favored by illustrators and comic artists. It also has 3D figure templates that can be manipulated for perfect anatomy and perspective. With customizable brushes, amazing vector capabilities, and a vast library of resources shared by its community, it's fantastic for character art, comics, and animation. However, Clip Studio Paint can be complex to use and might take some time to get accustomed to.

3.7. Corel Painter

Corel Painter is aimed at artists looking for a software that mimics traditional art media. It's fantastic for creating digital art that looks incredibly similar to physical paintings. From watercolor to oil paint, pastels, and charcoal, every medium has a realistic and organic feel with unique textures and behavior. Also, this tool offers a huge variety of brushes and customization options, although it can be quite resource-intensive on your system.

In conclusion, the choice of art software largely depends on your specific needs and preference. Beginners might lean towards tools with a more accessible interface, like Procreate or Sketchbook, while professionals might prefer something more advanced like Photoshop or Corel Painter. Regardless of your choice, your creative journey in the digital paradigm is about to take flight. Remember, it's not just the software; it's the artist behind it that truly brings art to life. Happy creating!

Chapter 4. Sketching 101: Translating Your Ideas onto the Digital Canvas

We begin implanting our artistic vision into the digital realm by mastering the simple, yet eternally valued skill: sketching. Coming from traditional sketching or starting anew, this transition will transform the way you perceive and participate in the creative process.

4.1. Getting Familiar with Digital Tools

As we embark on our sketching journey, the first step is to familiarize ourselves with the medium: digital tools. To create sketches, several digital softwares are available. Industry standards include tools like Adobe Photoshop, Corel Painter, and Autodesk Sketchbook. These platforms all feature sketching-friendly tools such as pencils, erasers, and shapes.

For tablet users, Procreate and Autodesk Sketchbook work wonders. Tablets with digital pencils enable more direct control, best mimicking the process of traditional sketching. For those without tablets, fear not, as using a mouse can also accomplish impressive sketches.

4.2. Understanding Sketching Basics

Sharpen your digital pencil, and let's begin! Sketching principally follows a similar path no matter the medium. We commence with broad strokes to outline our subject's general shape – this method, otherwise known as mark making, is about putting ideas down quickly.

Let's start by blocking out our subject's basic forms. Are we sketching a face? Then, start by outlining an oval or round form, go ahead to mark the eye line, nose, and mouth positions. Technicalities come in later; at this stage, your marks need not be precise.

Next, we refine our subject: make the outline more explicit, structure the facial features, and give dimension to your subject. Here, we introduce two essential techniques: hatching and cross-hatching. Hatching is drawing parallel lines to create the illusion of shadow and depth, while cross-hatching overlaps these lines at an angle to intensify the effect.

In sketching, we need to remember one key technique: the use of line weight. Line weight refers to how thick or thin lines are - thicker lines will appear closer and vice versa; they also highlight essential areas while silhouetting your drawing.

4.3. Layers: The Magic of Digital Sketching

The principal advantage of digital sketching is the ability to use layers. Think of layers as clear sheets stacked on top of each other, where you can draw different parts of your sketch. This way, if you make a mistake or decide to alter something, just that layer is affected, not your entire sketch.

A good practice is to draw your initial sketch or draft on one layer. As you refine your sketch, add a new layer aiming for finer details. Continue to use multiple layers for shading, coloring, and additional detailing. Your layering will depend on your personal preference and workflow.

4.4. Practicing and Developing Your Style

As Pablo Picasso said, "I am always doing that which I cannot do, in order that I may learn how to do it." Sketching, like any other skill, needs practice. The more you sketch, the more comfortable you become with digital tools, and your style will naturally develop.

To help nurture these skills, dedicate regular time to sketching and explore different subjects, from still life to the human figure, landscapes, and abstract forms. Experiment with different techniques and tool settings. Learn from others: the internet is brimming with talented artists who share their knowledge and skills.

4.5. Concluding Remarks

In conclusion, transitioning to sketching on a digital canvas may seem daunting initially, but with a curious mind and steadfast patience, you will lay down roots in digital sketching swiftly. Remember, the secret to improvement is to practice consistently, learn zealously, and never shy away from making mistakes. As we continue to explore this digital art landscape, we unlock the immense creative possibilities it holds. This is just the beginning of our journey.

Chapter 5. Basics of Color Theory: Painting with Pixels

Decoding the language of colors is the first step in any artistic journey. Colors can speak in whispers and shouts, carrying the power to evoke emotions and tell your story. In digital painting, this language takes on a unique dimension. In our journey, we'll cover a variety of topics, including primary colors, secondary colors, complementary colors, warm and cool colors, and then dip our brushes into color harmonies and the use of color in digital painting.

5.1. Understanding Primary Colors

Waltz into the world of color with the absolute basics- primary colors. These are the three fundamental colors that cannot be created by mixing others. They are red, blue, and yellow, akin to the three primary numbers of color, the building blocks from which the entire numerical system (or in case, the color wheel) is created.

When painting digitally, a slightly modified version of the primary colors—red, green, and blue (RGB)—is used. This is simply because digital screens emit light, not reflected light like tangible paint does. Hence, the primary colors shift, better suited to the medium.

5.2. Rendezvous with Secondary Colors

Secondary colors are born by blending any two primary colors. They are equidistant from the primaries on the color wheel, a child of two different primary-color parents:

- Red and blue birth purple.

- Blue and green generate cyan.

- Red and green concoct yellow.

Try blending different primary colors on your digital canvas and observe the secondary colors burgeon.

5.3. Unfolding Complementary Colors

Next, we take two steps forward into the realm of complementary colors. These are the pairings that sit directly opposite each other on the color wheel, and when they meet, they intensify each other. For example, green complements red, and orange complements blue.

When used together in your digital artwork, they provoke a dynamic that can breathe life into your creation. Used well, they can steer your viewer's focus where you desire and enhance the aesthetic value of your work. But be warned, too much use can lead to color chaos.

5.4. Warm vs Cool Colors

Colors also carry temperature! We divide these into warm (red, orange, yellow) and cool colors (blue, green, violet). Warm colors are radiant and energetic, often associated with light, heat, and day. In contrast, cool colors are calming and soothing, evoking the tranquility of a forest or the depth of an ocean.

Strategically implementing temperature can dictate the emotional tone of your digital art.

5.5. Introduction to Color Harmonies

Delving deeper into color theory, we encounter color harmonies. These are combinations of colors that provide a pleasing contrast yet possess an aesthetic unity that is visually appealing:

- **Monochromatic Harmony:** This involves tints, tones, and shades of a single hue.

- **Analogue Colors:** These are colors adjacent to each other on the color wheel.

- **Triadic Harmony:** This includes three colors evenly spaced on the color wheel.

Experiment with these harmonies in your digital artistry to create mood and form attractive focal points.

5.6. The Dance of Color in the Digital World

Digital painting, an advancement of our age, possesses its unique language of color. Colors in digital painting can be adjusted with unparalleled precision using the numerically driven RGB spectrum or HEX codes. Layer modes interacting with colors offer new depth to explore- enabling bright light overlays, deep multiplies, and color-burn effects.

Remember to keep your digital palette organized; managing a library of used colors can significantly aid in maintaining color harmony and consistency. Furthermore, the 'undo' feature allows you to test colors without the fear of irrevocable actions.

5.7. Using Color to Convey Meaning

Art is a form of communication, and color, its language. Every hue has specific connotations and can trigger a range of emotions. For example, red can denote romance or danger, while blue might suggest tranquility or melancholy. By tactfully employing colors in your digital art, you can connect with your viewers on a profound level, playing their emotions like keys on a piano.

Colors have the potential to define the essence of your digital painting, constructing an atmosphere, implying space and depth, or directing attention. A good understanding of color theory lays the groundwork on which to build your painting's narrative.

Parting with this chapter's knowledge, keep in mind that color theory is a guide, not a set of rigid rules. Like every technique and tool in art, color is an immersive journey, an exploration. As illustrator Stanley Meltzoff once said: "Paintings are but research and experiment. I never do a painting as a work of art. All of them are researches. I search constantly and there is a logical sequence in all this research."

Chapter 6. Exploring Art Styles: From Realism to Surrealism in the Digital Sphere

Digital art, a medium as diverse as the artists who wield it, provides an avenue to explore myriad art styles. Within this realm, no two are identical – each carries its own unique elements and spirit. The journey starts from the classic era of Realism, paving the way through the mind-bending realm of Surrealism.

6.1. Realism

Realism originated in the mid-19th century, an era that witnessed a decisive turn from romanticism and excess grandeur. It focused on portraying the world "as it is," without sugarcoating or glorifying. In the realm of digital art, replicating realism can be a powerful exercise to develop observational skills and refine techniques.

Start by honing your observational skills. Keep a keen eye on your surroundings, capturing minute details, right from the texture of a leaf to the subtle play of light and shadow on an object. Digital art platforms offer the tools like airbrush, digital pen, and pencils to simulate the intricate details found in a realistic style of art.

To practice, find reference images, or better yet, sit by an open window and capture the world beyond. Strive to replicate what you see as authentically as possible - the more accurate the shapes, the colors, the shading, and the lighting, the more realistic your work will look.

6.2. Impressionism

Impressionism, borne out the mid-19th century in France, was characterized by capturing the sensory impressions of a scene rather than its details. Impressionist artists strive to convey the feeling and mood of a moment, often using loose brushwork and vibrant colors.

Digitally, impressionism can be mimicked using a variety of tools. Opt for brush tools with softer and more diffuse edges, and use a less saturated color palette to depict the scene's light and mood rather than detailing it meticulously. Experiment with speed painting techniques as they mirror the characteristic spontaneity of impressionism.

6.3. Expressionism

In the early 20th century, expressionism took center stage, an art style focused on showcasing the artist's subjective emotions and responses. It's less about the realistic representation and more about the emotional impact. Bold colors, distorted forms, and gestural marks are the trademarks of expressionistic digital art.

Expressive digital painting is all about letting your emotions pilot your "brush". Choose color palettes that align with your feelings. Apply strokes liberally and experiment with the warp or twist tools to distort your forms and create that emotional turmoil typical of this style.

6.4. Cubism and Abstract Art

In the spotlight during the early 20th century, cubism, pioneered by Pablo Picasso and Georges Braque, radically upended conventional forms. It introduced multiple viewpoints in a single painting, primarily through geometric shapes.

Abstract art, on the other hand, does away with the need to represent an accurate depiction of visual reality. It emphasizes lines, colors, forms, and their interplay to create compositions that may exist solely for their aesthetic or evocative power.

In digital art, both cubism and abstract art can be rendered integrating geometric shapes tool, layering techniques, and bold, contrasting colors. Here, the focus should be less on depicting a reality, but more on playing with form and color to elicit an emotional or intellectual response.

6.5. Surrealism

Finally, we arrive at surrealism, an artistic revolution from the 1920s. It aimed to liberate the mind by defying reason and convention, often involving dreamlike, bizarre, or even illogical elements.

Creating surreal digital art can be thrilling, as it dares you to think "outside the box". Incorporate unexpected elements, play with scale and proportion, and use juxtapositions that surprise your audience. The lasso, transform and warp tools come in handy when attempting this art style.

An understanding and exploration of these varied art styles can not only educate a budding digital artist about art history but also equip them with varied techniques, broadening their creative skills. Remember, it's always rewarding to experiment with different styles, thereby developing your unique digital vocabulary in this ever-evolving art world. The journey of art learning is an ongoing process – always remain inquisitive, be bold in your exploration, and let your creativity flow unhindered.

Chapter 7. Texture and Shades: Creating Depth and Dimension

Open your mind to the realm of Texture and Shades, the twins of artistic depth and dimension. In the universe of digital art, they are far more than simple elements. They are, in essence, the very tools by which you can create lifelike representations, swirling narratives, and stunning vistas. Texture and shades dictate how real an object will look, the way it will reflect and absorb light, and interact visually with other elements of your design.

7.1. Understanding Texture and Shades

Texture in digital art is the perceived surface quality of an artwork. It provides the visual sensation of touch without physical contact. It suggests how an object or environment might feel—sharp, rough, soft, smooth, and more. Colors, lines, and shapes can all contribute to creating texture. Similarly, shading dictates how light interacts with the objects and environments in your art. By adjusting colors and tones, we add depth and volume to a piece.

In digital art, both texture and shade can be achieved through a variety of techniques and tools. Most art software like Adobe Photoshop, ProCreate, or Clip Studio Paint offer texture brushes, which simulate different types of textures. In terms of shading, the gradient tool, blending modes, and layers are commonly used to achieve the desired result. Some apps like Procreate also have smudging tools that are perfect for blending.

7.2. Incorporating Textures in Your Art

Looking for ways to add texture is like starting an exciting treasure hunt. The world is brim-full of textures. From the roughness of a rock to the smoothness of silk, there's a vast array of textures to explore and incorporate into your art.

Initial steps begin by understanding the effect a texture will have on your image. If you're creating a cozy scene, for instance, softer, warmer textures, like fur or cloth, might be appropriate. Conversely, a more industrial setting may require harder, cooler textures, like metal or concrete. Once you've thought about the types of textures you want to include, it's time to add them to your artwork.

Most digital art programs allow you to create your own brushes. These can simulate the textures you want to implement. You can also use pre-existing brushes in art programs, or use a blending tool to create a simulated texture. Artists often layer multiple brush strokes and different shades of color to create a highly textured effect. Also, using different brush strokes patterns can add to the textural diversity of your piece.

7.3. Mastering the Art of Shading

Shading is crucial for bringing your artwork to life. It adds depth and gives your objects dimension, making them appear three-dimensional. While mastering shading isn't an overnight process, with practice and patience, you can create impressive effects.

Shading often involves choosing a light source and sticking with it. You need to know where your light is coming from to understand where the highlights and shadows will go. Most importantly, consistency is key. Picking multiple light sources can make your image look chaotic and unrealistic.

To begin shading, decide your base color first. Then, choose a tone darker for the shadow parts and a tone brighter for the highlighted parts. Depending on how intense the light source is, you can decide the degree of difference between the original and the dark or light tone. Make use of layers, blending tools, or gradients to make the transition of colors gradual and thus, more realistic.

And remember, it's crucial to familiarize yourself with how different textures respond to light. A shiny metal surface will interact with light differently than a matte piece of cloth. Don't be afraid to study from real life and photos, as understanding how light interacts with objects in the real world will hugely benefit your digital art.

7.4. Experimenting to Find Your Style

Every digital artist has a unique approach to incorporating textures and shades into their work. It's all about finding what appeals to you, and what resonates with your artistic instincts. Don't be afraid to play around with different textures, brushes, blending modes, and shading techniques. Sometimes, it's through trial and error that we discover our style.

Whether you are exploring the digital art world's intricacies or diving deeper to enhance your skills, remember that progress takes time. Embrace the process, keep learning and experimenting, and never forget the joy that the journey of creativity brings to you. Also, connect with peers or join online digital art communities; their shared experiences can provide valuable insights and inspiration.

With this in-depth understanding of texture and shades, prepare to bid farewell to flat, lifeless artworks. Breathing life and adding depth and dimension to your digital creations is now at your fingertips. So embrace these techniques of texture and shades, and watch your digital art journey skyrocket to captivating heights. Happy creating!

Chapter 8. Mastering Digital Brushes: Bring Life to Your Art

This chapter will step you through the vast world of digital brushes, sharing practical, accessible insights that will help you wield the most versatile tool in any digital artist's arsenal.

8.1. Understanding Brushes and Their Properties

At first glance, digital brushes may seem daunting because of their variety, but understanding their properties can make them your best friends in the world of digital art!

1. **Shape / Tip**: The shape or tip of the brush defines the footprint the brush will leave on your canvas. Each program has its range of default shapes, but you can customize your brushes or download additional shapes. Some software allows importing brushes, enhancing your toolset.

2. **Size**: This adjusts the diameter of your brush tip. Remember, larger brushes can cover more space, but smaller ones offer precision.

3. **Flow**: Determines how quickly paint is laid down. Lower flow rates mean that less paint is applied each time you pass over a stroke, allowing for gradual buildup.

4. **Opacity**: Controls how transparent your brush stroke will be. A lower opacity means a more transparent stroke.

5. **Hardness**: This alters the sharpness of the brush edge. Hard brushes have crisp edges, while soft brushes fade out from the

center to the edges.

6. **Spacing**: This controls the gap between brush marks in a stroke. Higher spacing results in a dotted line, while lower spacing creates a smooth stroke.

8.2. Choosing the Right Brush

Just like traditional artists choose different brushes for various effects, your choice in the digital world should correspond to the result you desire.

1. **Round brushes**: These are the most versatile and commonly used digital brushes. You can use them for sketching, coloring, or soft shading, adjusting their hardness and opacity according to your need.

2. **Airbrushes**: They simulate the traditional airbrush and are great for creating gradients or soft shadows.

3. **Texture brushes**: These come in handy when you want to add details, like the texture of fur or the grain of wood.

4. **Special effect brushes**: These brushes are used for particular effects like creating stars, flames, rain, or any abstract element.

Remember, you can often mix and layer different kinds of brushes to achieve your desired effect!

8.3. Techniques to Bring Life to Your Art

1. **Layering colors**: Apply colors in multiple layers to create depth and dimension. Start with a lower opacity and gradually build up the intensity.

2. **Blending**: Soft edges and smooth transitions can be achieved by

using digital brushes to blend colors together.

3. **Stippling**: This involves making numerous small dots or specks to create textures or tone areas.

4. **Hatching and Cross-Hatching**: Creating close parallel lines (hatching), or layering them at an angle (cross-hatching), can convey value and texture.

5. **Dry Brushing**: By setting a low flow rate and high spacing, you can create a 'dry brush' effect – perfect for textures or to give a vintage look to your art.

8.4. Tips to Improve Your Brush Work

1. **Play with Pressure Sensitivity**: If you're painting with a stylus, adjust the pressure sensitivity for more control over the thickness and opacity of your strokes.

2. **Customize brushes**: Experiment with altering the properties of your digital brushes or creating your own to achieve unique effects.

3. **Shortcut Keys**: Mastering shortcut keys for changing brush size or opacity on the fly can make your painting process quicker and smother.

4. **Practice**: Just like traditional painting, digital art requires practice. Spend time doodling and experimenting to understand what each brush can do.

5. **Clean your Canvas Regularly**: Too many strokes can make your artwork look muddy. Erase or undo strokes that don't contribute to your piece.

In the dazzling journey of digital art, brushes are your magic wand. They can create bold lines, soft blurs, textured patterns, and in fact, a whole universe expressing your unique artistic style. Experience the joy of paint flying off brushes, exclusively catering to your command, and watch as the canvas of your imagination comes alive. Breathe, blush, and brush on! The masterpiece within you is all set to blaze into a stirring saga! Let the colors of your soul splash and splatter! Dive into the splendid swirl of brushes and let creativity become your second nature.

Chapter 9. Layering Techniques: Crafting Complex Compositions

Art, like many aspects of life, is composed of different layers. Each layer adds depth and complexity to the overall composition, allowing the artist to experiment and improvise. In digital art, the concept of layering is even more instrumental, providing the flexibility to manipulate individual components without affecting the entire image. In this chapter, we will delve into the essential techniques of layering that help bring your art to life.

9.1. Understanding Layers

Let's start by defining what we mean by 'layers'. In digital artistry, think of layers as transparent sheets stacked on top of each other, each containing different elements of your artwork. Consider the layers as your art's different elements - the background, main character, surrounding objects, lighting effects, and shadows. Managing these aspects separately gives you the freedom to experiment without disturbing the other components. Now let's further investigate how these are used in digital compositions.

9.2. Layer Types and Their Uses

In most digital art software, you will find several layer types, each having a unique purpose. The common layer types include:

1. Normal: A standard layer where you can draw, erase or apply colors.

2. Multiply: This layer allows the colors beneath to show through, useful for shadows or darkening areas.

3. Screen: Brightens the colors underneath and is useful for highlights and light effects.

4. Overlay: Heavy-handed combination of multiply and screen, which intensifies the colors underneath.

5. Adjustment Layers: Non-destructive edits like Brightness/Contrast, Hue/Saturation, Levels, and Curves can be applied through this layer.

Whether you are drawing a dramatic manga character or designing a dreamy landscape, knowing how to utilize these layers can drastically enhance your work.

9.3. Managing Layers

Organizing layers is essential for a clean and manageable workspace. It allows for a structured workflow, especially when dealing with complex compositions with numerous elements. You can group similar layers, such as all those associated with character design or background elements and label each group. This way, you will save time and avoid confusion when jumping between layers.

9.4. Layer Transparency and Blending Modes

Manipulating layer transparency and blending modes is a powerful technique to create intricate and vivid images. You can adjust layer opacity to create transparency effects – think of a ghostly apparition or reflecting water. Blending modes like multiply, screen, hard light, overlay, etc., multiply, or mix the pixel values of your layer with the ones beneath, providing rich and complex visual effects.

9.5. Shadow and Light Effects Using Layers

Crafting a realistic or dramatic light effect can make your artwork stand out. Using layers, you can create an array of lights and shadows, from subtle to very stark, to give your work a sense of volume and depth. Delicate lighting can be achieved using screen or add layers while multiply layers can cast deep shadows.

9.6. Layer Masks

A layer mask is an incredibly flexible tool. It allows you to hide and reveal parts of your layer without permanently erasing them. It's a non-destructive way of editing an image, which means you can always change your mind and undo your actions without losing any work.

9.7. Adjustment Layers

As mentioned earlier, adjustment layers are a type of layer that applies color and tonal adjustments to your image without permanently changing pixel values. You can correct the coloring of your art, increase or decrease contrast and brightness, change saturation levels, and adjust curves and levels to modify the mood and feel of your entire piece or certain parts of your artwork.

9.8. Filters and Layer Styles

Filters allow you to apply effects to a single layer, a group of layers, or even your entire canvas, adding textures or creating visual illusions such as motion blur or noise. Layer styles also provide options to create effects like drop shadow, outer glow, emboss, etc. These add a whole new dimension to your digital art toolkit.

9.9. Some Layering Tips

Mediocre layers lead to mediocre artworks. Here are a few tips to elevate your layering game:

1. Keep your layers organized: This simple practice preserves sanity. Name and group them properly for faster navigation.

2. Use shortcut keys: Learn the shortcut keys of your digital art software to achieve quick layering actions.

3. Understand blending modes: The right blending mode can add a wow factor to your artwork.

4. Preserve original layers: Before applying filters or adjustments, duplicate the original layer to preserve it.

Layering is like the scaffolding for digital artwork – structural, necessary, and temporarily hidden until the masterpiece is ready. These techniques may seem daunting at first, but with practice, you will grow to appreciate the flexibility and creativity that layering provides. So grab your digital brushes, experiment with layers, and let your imagination soar!

Chapter 10. Introduction to Digital Animation: Moving Beyond Static

It's no secret that a well-drawn and static image can be stunning, but imagine how much more impacting and exciting it could be if that image started moving. Creating animations gives your artwork life, turning your creations into a magical world filled with vibrant characters, expressive emotions, and action-packed scenes. Welcome to the exciting realm of digital animation!

10.1. Why Digital Animation?

The magic of digital animation allows us to bring our imaginations to life, taking our art to a different dimension that transcends the static nature of traditional artwork. It is a tool that can turn your simple sketches into lively characters and transform your still backgrounds into vibrant landscapes. The increased digitalization and advanced software available today make learning digital animation more feasible and exciting for everyone, especially teens like you, with a unique blend of creativity and tech-sensitivity.

Animation serves a variety of purposes far beyond just entertainment. It's used in biology to illustrate how cells divide, in architecture to create 3D renderings of buildings, and even in education to make complex concepts easier to understand. The skills and techniques you learn in digital animation can offer you a wide range of opportunities in various fields.

10.2. Getting Started: Software and Tools

To get started in digital animation, you'll need the right tools. While there are numerous free and paid animation software programs on the market, some of the most popular for beginners include Adobe Animate, Toon Boom Harmony, and Blender. These programs offer an easy-to-navigate interface and a plethora of resources to help you learn the ropes.

In addition to the software, having a graphics tablet can make the animation process much more comfortable and intuitive. Instead of using a mouse to draw on your computer, you can use a stylus on a tablet specific for drawing, which greatly improves control and flexibility.

10.3. Understanding the Basics: Frames and Timeline

One of the core principles of digital animation is mastering the concept of frames and timeline. An animation, in its simplest form, is a series of still images shown in rapid succession. Each of these images is known as a 'frame'. The quicker these frames change, the smoother your animation will appear.

The timeline is where you'll manage these frames. It's the section of your animation software where you will add, remove, and manipulate frames to create movement. Understanding how to control the timeline is crucial for creating an effective and smooth animation.

10.4. Achieving Motion: The Power of Keyframes

To create motion in animation, we employ a tool called 'Keyframes'. Keyframes are the points of change in an animation. For instance, if you want a ball to move across the screen, you would create two keyframes: one for the starting position and one for the ending position. The software will create the frames in between, a process known as 'Tweening', providing a smooth transition from one keyframe to the next.

10.5. Bringing Characters to Life: Animation Techniques

There are several techniques used in animation that help bring movement and personality to your characters. Two of the core methods are 'Squash and Stretch' and 'Anticipation'.

'Squash and Stretch' is a technique that involves changing the shape of an object or character to exaggerate its motion. For example, a ball will squash when it hits the ground and stretch as it bounces up.

'Anticipation' is used to prepare the viewer for a major action the character is about to perform, such as jumping or running. This could be a backward movement before jumping forward or a wind-up motion before throwing an object.

10.6. Conclusion

Animation is more than just moving images. It's a form of art that breathes life into your creations, making them interactive and relatable. It opens up an endless world of creativity where your visions can leap from your mind to a dynamic world where they can dance, run, smile, or even fly. As with any art form, it takes practice and patience to hone your skills. So, don't be discouraged if your first few animations look choppy or raw. With every stroke, with every frame, you're setting a stepping-stone towards transforming your versatile ideas into the dancing hues of digital animation magic.

By the end of our journey together, you'll have a solid foundation of digital animation basics and a hands-on understanding of animation software. And most importantly, you'll have the thrill and pride that comes from watching your artworks come alive. Now, let's get ready to animate!

Chapter 11. The Future of Digital Art: Trends and Career Opportunities

As we navigate forward in the world of digital art, one thing is irrefutable: its future is bright and filled with possibilities. Digital art has not only revolutionized the way we create art but has also redefined career avenues for young, budding artists. This beacon of creativity lights up our ideas, giving them fresh dimensions embedded in technology.

11.1. The Evolution of Digital Art

From its humble beginnings in the 1980s, when it was primarily a tool for enhancing traditional artwork, digital art has traversed a spectacular journey. Today, it's an artistic entity in itself. Early digital art required artists to type numerical codes on punch cards, which a mainframe computer then translated into a visual piece on the printout. It was the invention of graphical user interfaces, including the mouse and bitmap graphics, that powered the evolution. Thanks to such advancements, creating digital artwork became accessible to artists on personal computers, ushering in a new era of digital creativity.

Holography and algorithm-generated art were also popular forms of digital art in the initial days. Over time, movable graphics and digital video art started becoming popular. Then came the fascinating world of 3D modelling, followed by the highly immersive virtual and augmented reality art. Today, we continue to see evolutions with technologies like artificial intelligence and machine learning driving the creation of new digital artwork.

11.2. Recent Trends in Digital Art

Artists now use software tools, such as Adobe Illustrator and Photoshop, Corel Painter, Autodesk Sketchbook Pro, and open-source software like GIMP and Inkscape, to create exquisite masterpieces. 3D applications like Blender, Maya and ZBrush are used for creating mesmerizing animations and models.

One of the most noteworthy trends in the world of digital art in recent times has been the explosion of Non-Fungible Tokens (NFTs). These crypto-based assets hold the value of digital art and can be bought and sold just like traditional art. NFTs have democratized the digital art world and empowered artists by providing them a direct and independent platform for their creations.

A blend of technology and art, Virtual Reality (VR) and Augicollection of digitallmented Reality (AR) produce an immersive experience for the viewer, which is truly a treat for the senses. Many museums and exhibitions are now offering VR and AR experiences to their visitors.

Digital Collage is another popular trend, using a collection of digital images, textures and photographs to create a new image. It's a poignant method of storytelling, offering limitless potential for creativity.

11.3. Career Opportunities in Digital Art

A career in digital art offers a dynamic, evolving landscape filled with exciting opportunities and creative rewards. Here are some of the great roles up for grabs:

1. Digital Illustrator: A professional who uses digital tools to create artwork for books, magazines, and websites. They are highly sought after in sectors like advertising, publishing, multimedia

design, and fashion.

2. Graphic Designer: They employ a blend of text and visual imagery to convey specific messages. Their skills are essential in sectors such as advertising, public relations, and media and communications.

3. 3D Artist: These professionals sculpt, render, and animate using 3D modeling programs. Typically, they work in film, gaming, interior design, and architecture industries.

4. Concept Artist: Often employed within the film, game, and animations industries, these artists visualize ideas and bring them to life.

5. Art Director: They oversee the creation of visual material for print, multimedia, and digital outlets. They are the key decision-makers in advertising, public relations, and multimedia industries.

6. Multimedia Artist: They use various forms of media to communicate specific messages or narratives. They often work in advertising, public relations, and the software creation sector.

11.4. Preparing For a Career in Digital Art

Securing a future in digital art needs an intricate combination of technical proficiency, creativity, practice, and passion. Startups and tech conglomerates are always seeking talented individuals who can think outside the box, bringing a fusion of arts and technology. There are various online and offline art courses and degree programs available that can provide you a strong foundation.

Moreover, it's crucial to build a solid portfolio to showcase your skill and range to potential employers. Enter exhibitions and competitions, which could be an excellent way to get your work noticed. Develop your brand on social media platforms to expand your network and make connections in the industry.

Digital Art, with its boundless opportunities, is a vibrant field for those aspiring to an innovative, technology-driven career. It is a world where your creative expression can take form in countless ways while adding value to the multifaceted canvas of the digital world. Unleash your creative potential, and the world will be your canvas!

Remember, as Vincent Van Gogh once said, "I dream of painting and then I paint my dream." Your aspirations can shape the future of digital art. Swing open the door to your dreams and step into the brilliant light of digital artistry.